The Bear on the Stairs

By Kathryn Harper

Illustrated by Paul Meisel

OXFORD

UNIVERSITY PRESS

Before you read, write the colours.

1 _____ door

2 _____ bath

3 _____ boat

4 _____ stairs

GERRY comes home from school
At five past four.
Grandpa always waits
By the big blue door.

He says:
'Tell me what you have to say.
Tell me what is new today.'

door

grandpa

home

school

On Monday Gerry says:
'There's a giraffe
Having a bath
On the path.'

Grandpa says:
'A giraffe on the path?
That's not true,
That cannot be.
There's no giraffe,
You're fooling me.'

It's a little joke,
It's so funny!
There's no giraffe,
Hee hee hee!

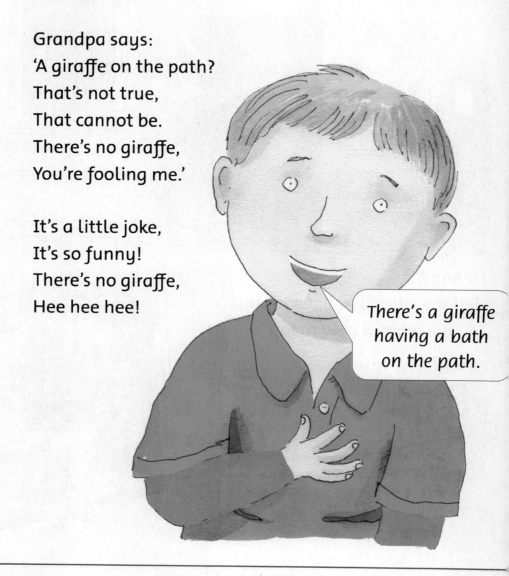

There's a giraffe having a bath on the path.

bath

funny

giraffe

path

On Tuesday Gerry says:
'There's a snake
Eating cake
In the lake.'

Grandpa says:
'A snake in the lake?
That's not true,
That cannot be.
There's no snake,
You're fooling me.'

It's a little joke,
It's so funny!
There's no snake,
Hee hee hee!

There's a snake eating cake in the lake.

cake

lake

snake

Find the words and write.

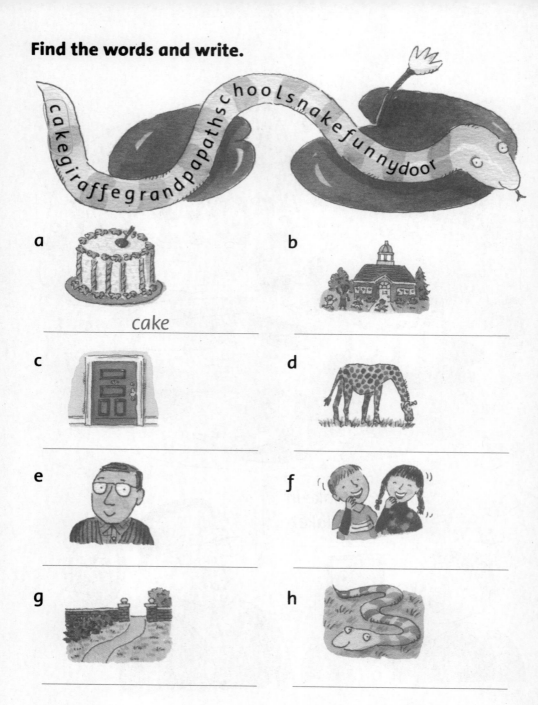

a

cake

b

c

d

e

f

g

h

Match the rhyming words.

snake

four

bath

lake

door

path

On Wednesday Gerry says:
'There's a goat
In a coat
In a boat!'

Grandpa says:
'A goat in a boat?
That's not true,
That cannot be.
There's no goat,
You're fooling me.'

It's a little joke,
It's so funny!
There's no goat,
Hee hee hee!

boat

coat

goat

On Thursday Gerry says:
'There's a fox
Selling socks
On the rocks!'

Grandpa says:
'A fox on the rocks?
That's not true,
That cannot be.
There's no fox,
You're fooling me.'

It's a little joke,
It's so funny!
There's no fox,
Hee hee hee!

There's a fox selling socks on the rocks!

fox

rocks

socks

What's missing in the pictures? Write.

cake   ~~socks~~   bath   coat

_____socks_____

_____

_____

_____

Circle the odd-one-out and write the words.

1

door

2

_____

3

_____

4

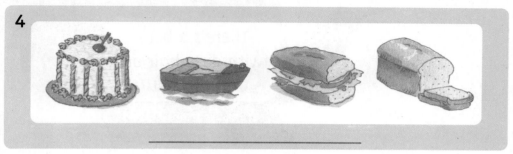

_____

On Friday Gerry says:
'There's a bear
With dirty hair
On the stairs!'

Grandpa says:
'A bear on the stairs?
That's not true,
That cannot be.
There's no bear,
You're fooling me.'

Gerry says:
'No, listen to me!
I'm not fooling you.
There's a bear on the stairs,
It's true, it's true!'

> There's a bear
> with dirty hair on
> the stairs!

bear	dirty	hair	stairs

Grandpa says:
'I'm old,
But I know a lot.
I know what's true
And what is not.'

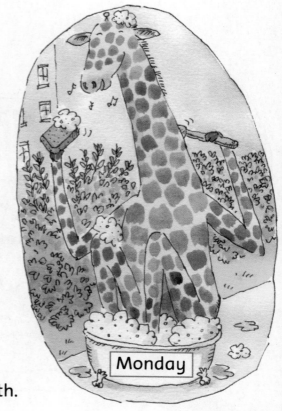

Monday

Tuesday

'On Monday
A giraffe on the path.
On Tuesday
A snake in the lake.
On Wednesday
A goat in a boat.
On Thursday
A fox on the rocks.
And now, on Friday
A bear on the stairs.
Hee hee hee, you can't fool me.
That's what I call make believe.'

Wednesday

Socks for Sale

Thursday

Friday

Gerry says:
'I'm not fooling.
Not this time.
I'm scared of that bear
And I'm really not lying.'

lie

make believe
(not real)

scared

Write the days of the week.

1 _____Thursday_____

2 _____

3 _____

4 _____

5 _____

What colour are the things in the story?

1 Gerry's T-shirt is _____*red*_____ .

2 The bear is _____ .

3 The snake is _____
and _____ .

4 The door is _____ .

5 The giraffe is _____
and _____ .

Grandpa says:
'Do you hear that great big roar?
Is that Miss McKay from the second floor?'

Gerry says:
'No. That isn't a woman
Or even a man.
It's a bear on the stairs.
Let's get out if we can.'

floor

man

roar

woman

Then there's a knock on the door.
It's Mr Smith from the seventh floor:
'Pardon me, don't be upset.
There's an animal on the stairs – it isn't a pet.'

animal

knock

pet

upset

The firemen come and then the police.
There's Mrs Baker and her nosey niece.
They want to look and have a stare
At the bear on the stairs with dirty hair.

Now there's a zookeeper on his bike,
And there's another – called Mike.
He's got a bag on a large brown trolley.
He takes out an enormous pink lolly!

lolly nosey trolley zookeeper

The bear on the stairs sees the sweet,
And in one second she's on her feet.
She jumps into the trolley — weeee!
And eats the lolly — one, two, three!

'Sorry, sorry,' the zookeepers say.
'It's bath time at the zoo today.
This bear sees soap and she runs away,
But come and visit another day.'

feet   soap   sweet   zoo

Gerry says:
'You see, Grandpa,
I know it's a surprise,
But I can tell the truth
And I don't always lie.'

Grandpa says:
'But it's not good if you say
One or two lies every day.
Here's an idea — take a good look —
When you talk, tell the truth
And write your stories in this book.'

story   surprise    tell the truth

Number the pictures in order and tell the story.

Gerry comes
home from school.

Write the words. Find the animal in the puzzle.

1

2

3

4

5

6

7

8

1	b	e	a	r

Act the play.

Scene 1

Narrator	On Monday Gerry comes home from school At five past four. Grandpa always waits By the big blue door.
Grandpa	Tell me what you have to say. Tell me what is new today.
Gerry	There's a giraffe having a bath On the path.
Grandpa	A giraffe on the path? That's not true, that cannot be.
Gerry	You're right. It's not true. There's no giraffe. I'm fooling you.
Narrator	On Tuesday Gerry comes home from school.
Grandpa	Tell me what you have to say. Tell me what is new today.
Gerry	There's a snake eating cake In the lake.
Grandpa	A snake in the lake? That's not true, that cannot be.
Gerry	You're right. It's not true. There's no snake. I'm fooling you.
Narrator	On Wednesday Gerry comes home from school.
Grandpa	Tell me what you have to say. Tell me what is new today.

Gerry	There's a goat in a boat
	Wearing a coat.
Grandpa	A goat in a boat?
	That's not true, that cannot be.
Gerry	You're right. It's not true.
	There's no goat. I'm fooling you.
Narrator	On Thursday Gerry comes home from school.
Grandpa	Tell me what you have to say.
	Tell me what is new today.
Gerry	There's a fox selling socks
	On the rocks!
Grandpa	A fox on the rocks?
	That's not true, that cannot be.
Gerry	You're right. It's not true.
	There's no fox. I'm fooling you.'
Narrator	On Friday Gerry comes home from school.
Grandpa	Tell me what you have to say.
	Tell me what is new today.
Gerry	There's a bear with dirty hair
	On the stairs!
Grandpa	A bear on the stairs?
	That's not true, that cannot be.
Gerry	No, listen to me! I'm not fooling you.
	There's a bear on the stairs,
	It's true, it's true.

Scene 2

Bear	ROAR!
Grandpa	Do you hear that great big roar?
	Is that Miss McKay from the second floor?
Gerry	No. That isn't a woman or even a man.
	It's a bear on the stairs, let's get out if we can.
Narrator	Then there's a knock on the door.
	It's Mr Smith from the seventh floor.
Mr Smith	Pardon me, don't be upset.
	There's an animal on the stairs – it isn't a pet.
Bear	ROAR!
Narrator	The firemen come and then the police.
	There's Mrs Baker and her nosey niece.
	They want to look and have a stare
	At the bear on the stairs with dirty hair.
Zookeepers	Sorry, sorry,
	It's washing time at the zoo today.
	The bear sees soap and she runs away!

Scene 3

Gerry	You see, Grandpa, I know it's a surprise,
	But I can tell the truth, I don't always lie.'
Grandpa	Here's an idea – take a good look –
	When you talk, tell the truth
	And write your stories in this book.

OXFORD
UNIVERSITY PRESS

Great Clarendon Street, Oxford OX2 6DP

Oxford University Press is a department of the University of Oxford.
It furthers the University's objective of excellence in research, scholarship,
and education by publishing worldwide in

Oxford New York

Auckland Cape Town Dar es Salaam Hong Kong Karachi
Kuala Lumpur Madrid Melbourne Mexico City Nairobi
New Delhi Shanghai Taipei Toronto

With offices in

Argentina Austria Brazil Chile Czech Republic France Greece
Guatemala Hungary Italy Japan Poland Portugal Singapore
South Korea Switzerland Thailand Turkey Ukraine Vietnam

OXFORD and OXFORD ENGLISH are registered trade marks of
Oxford University Press in the UK and in certain other countries

ISBN: 978 0 19 480259 8

Printed in China

ACKNOWLEDGEMENTS
Story by: Kathryn Harper
Illustrated by: Paul Meisel / Tugeau 2 Inc.